P9-CBB-453

The Let's Talk Library

Let's Talk About Being Shy

Marianne Johnston

The Rosen Publishing Group's

PowerKids Press
New York

Published in 1996 by The Rosen Publishing Group, Inc.
29 East 21st Street, New York, NY 10010

Copyright © 1996 by The Rosen Publishing Group, Inc.

All rights reserved. No part of this book may be reproduced in any form without permission in writing from the publisher, except by a reviewer.

Photo credits: Cover photo © Maratea/International Stock; p. 8 © Robert Tulin/International Stock; p. 16 © Barry Elz/International Stock; p. 20 © Dusty Willison/International Stock; all other photos by Maria Moreno.

First Edition

Johnston, Marianne.
    Let's talk about being shy / Marianne Johnston. — 1st ed.
        p.   cm. — (The let's talk library)
    Includes index.
    Summary: Introduces the concept of shyness and offers suggestions on how to deal with it.
    ISBN 0-8239-2304-5
    1. Bashfulness in children—Juvenile literature. [1. Bashfulness.] I. Title. II. Series.
    BF723.B3J64   1996
    155.4'18232—dc20   95-50793
                                                    CIP
                                                        AC

Manufactured in the United States of America

Table of Contents

What Is Shyness?

Some people are very quiet. They don't seem to want to talk to other people very often. Are you sometimes afraid to talk to others?

Being quiet or feeling nervous around other people are signs of shyness. A shy person is very **cautious** (CAW-shus) in new situations and feels **uncomfortable** (un-KUM-for-ta-bul) meeting new people. Everyone feels shy sometimes. But being too shy can be harmful.

◀ A shy person usually doesn't feel comfortable around other people.

When Do People Feel Shy?

Do you feel shy when you meet someone new? Did you feel shy on your first day of school?

Some people are shy when they have to speak in front of a lot of people. Sometimes people are shy just going to the store to buy something. There are lots of times when people feel shy.

Many people feel shy when they have to speak in front of a group of people. ▶

Colin's First Day

Colin's first day at his new elementary school was scary. His family had just moved to a new town, and he didn't know anybody. He was so shy that he couldn't talk to anyone, not even his teacher.

But soon Colin got used to his new school. This helped him to get over his shyness, and in a few weeks Colin made new friends.

◀ It may take a little time to get over your shyness.

You're Not the Only One

Being shy doesn't mean there is something wrong with you. Almost everyone is shy sometimes.

Kids are usually more shy than grown-ups. As a kid, you're still learning all about the world around you.

The older you get and the more you learn, the less shy you will probably become.

As you grow older, you will probably become less shy. ▶

Why Are People Shy?

People are shy for lots of reasons. Some people don't like themselves very much, so they think others won't like them either.

Some people are shy because they have been teased or made fun of, and they are afraid it will happen again.

And some people are just naturally quiet, so they seem shy when someone tries to talk to them.

◀ Some people are shy because they are afraid they will be teased.

Caution Can Be Good

Being shy isn't always a bad thing. There are certain times when it helps to be a little shy or cautious. Being cautious can help you stay away from danger. When you are cautious, you look both ways before you cross the street at the crosswalk.

Being cautious can also help you avoid bad situations like talking to strangers.

No matter how friendly someone may look, it's good to be cautious of people you don't know. ▶

When Shyness Is Harmful

Being too shy can cause problems. Shyness can keep you from making new friends. It can keep you from doing new things, like joining a sports team or taking dance lessons.

Does your shyness stop you from trying new things or meeting new people? If the answer is yes, your shyness might be harmful to you.

◀ People who are too shy often end up spending a lot of time alone.

Try and Try Again

Some people are shy because they are afraid of **failure** (FAYL-yur), or making mistakes. When you were a baby, you couldn't walk on your first try. You fell down a lot and kept trying until you learned how to do it. Most things in life are just like that. You can't be perfect at something right away. But if you are too shy even to try, you will never know if you could have done it.

It takes time and practice to learn something new, like learning to walk. ▶

The Gymnast

Jen had always wanted to take gymnastics. But she was afraid to join a class because she was worried that she would fall off the balance beam.

Even though she was afraid, Jen joined a class. After just two weeks, she became one of the best gymnasts in the class. If she had let her shyness stop her, Jen never would have known what a good gymnast she was.

◀ It takes courage to overcome the fear of doing something new.

Low Self-Esteem

People who don't feel good about themselves have low **self-esteem** (SELF-es-TEEM). If you don't like yourself, you may think others won't like you either. This can make you feel or seem shy. The way to change this is to feel better about yourself. Think of some good things about yourself. Are you honest? Are you funny? When you feel good about yourself, you will want to be around other people, and you won't feel so shy.

Glossary

cautious (CAW-shus) Being careful in certain situations.

failure (FAYL-yur) Trying to do something and not being able to.

self-esteem (SELF-es-TEEM) How you feel about yourself.

uncomfortable (un-KUM-for-ta-bul) A feeling of uneasiness.

Index